ABOUT THE AUTHOR

Humberto Aguilar, also called Beto Guaymas

Born in the city of Guaymas, Sonora, Mexico.

The second of four children of a fishermen family, coming from a poor background, he paved his way through the rough pathways towards a successful career with utmost courage, devotion and determination.

Accountant, Computer Systems Engineer "Entitled with Honorably Mention" and Master´s in Tele-informatics.

Entrepreneur, lecturer, writer, and a philanthropist.

His passion for motivational strategies and teamwork has led him to discover the driving factors that encourage people depending on their country, culture, religion and socioeconomic background.

He has worked in over 30 countries which has helped him learn from their cultural, socioeconomic, educational and professional differences.

He invented a system for blind people in 2000 which was used by an 11 year old visually impaired girl who is currently a lawyer.

One of his ventures includes supporting the disabled community by offering professional employment to compete in the "normal" world.

He has won international awards for teamwork, sense of urgency, leadership, public speaking and business strategy.

He is also dedicated to mentoring emerging entrepreneurs so they can start their own venture or grow their existing businesses.

TABLE OF CONTENTS

PREFACE 6
ACKNOWLEDGMENTS 7
INTRODUCTION 8
Being an Employee "EmpleaT" 12
   Being an employee 13
   Being a great employee 15
   Meritocracy 21
   How to climb the ladder quickly 25
   Why don't GURUS climb the ladder? 27
   Time to change jobs 29
   How to take care of your employees so they don't leave 33
   Competitive employees 35
   Training 36
   No one is indispensable 39
   Degrees and qualifications do not make good employees 41
   Why do employees resign? 43
   Employee myths 44
   Does being an employee give you financial freedom? 47
ArriesgaT (Take Risk) 50
   Is a college degree necessary? 53

Traveling	55
Choosing the right people	57
Protect your essence, but don't repress it	59
Intra-entrepreneur	62
The leap from employee to entrepreneur	64
AdaptaT (Adaptation)	66
Learning entrepreneurship	68
When should you quit your job?	70
EmprendeT (Be an Entrepreneur)	73
When you are ready to be an entrepreneur?	73
When is the best time to be an entrepreneur?	76
When should you NOT start a venture?	78
Can anyone be an entrepreneur?	81
What is the best age for entrepreneurship?	83
A good idea	85
Failure; the best teacher	87
Being positive	89
Why does an entrepreneur fail?	92
Can you start a business without money?	96
Partners	100
How to choose a partner?	101
Common mistakes to avoid while choosing a partner:	103

Systematize your business	106
Business Plan	108
Right place	112
Attracting clients	114
The power of socializing	116
Dark side of entrepreneurship	117
The social game	120
Recommendations to reach success faster	123
Learn to say NO	124
Public Speaking	127
Create your habits	129
Advantages	129
Disadvantages	129
Create a good habit	129
Researchers	130
Entrepreneurial habit	131
Perfection is the enemy of an entrepreneur	132
Employee or Entrepreneur	134
Which one gives you financial freedom?	134

PREFACE

This book has been the compilation of my experiences in the field of work and entrepreneurship, as well as, the experiences that I have taken from a series of entrepreneurs and businessmen where I had the opportunity to interview in the program "Un Café para Emprender"; likewise I have taken experiences of entrepreneurs who have failed on multiple occasions and have turned their lives around emerging as successful entrepreneurs.

I have also filtered experiences of influencers of the moment who talk about entrepreneurship and it´s shortcuts that we should not let pass us by in order not to give false expectations to our entrepreneurs.

It has been a personal challenge that I decided to share with all those people who work in a company as employees and who also have the desire to be entrepreneurs at some point of their lives. I would like to share this book with all the entrepreneurs out there who are on this difficult, unknown and arduous path of entrepreneurship.

> "If you have a voice and you are heard, you better say something worthwhile and change someone's life".
>
> *Unknown*

ACKNOWLEDGMENTS

First of all, I would like to thank my wife, who has been the first person to support me, pushing me to live and capture all my work experiences as an entrepreneur; she has been the ultimate source of motivation which made me write this book.

To my children who put up with my absence, without knowing my whereabouts.

To the entrepreneurs, businessmen and great employees who contributed their experiences with me in the program "Un Café para Emprender", from which we compiled a lot of valuable information which is available in this book.

Thanks to all the companies that gave me the opportunity to collaborate as an employee, for having educated me and for all the challenges that made me grow. I would also like to thank the people who have trusted my professionalism and my experiences as an entrepreneur, which I now share with great pleasure.

INTRODUCTION
"EmpleaT o EmprendeT" (Be an Employee or an Entrepreneur)

The most frequent question I have been asked throughout my professional and entrepreneurial life is "Which is better, being an entrepreneur or being an employee?"

In the end it is a matter of perspective, what are you looking for out of life, what are your goals, where do you want to go, what would you like to achieve, what would you like to do, how much money would you like to make, what would you like to live on, and so on. A series of endless questions come out of my mind when I am questioned about that.

In my experience as an employee and/or entrepreneur I have realized that both are good and one can even beautifully complement the other.

However, it all depends on the focus with which you want to see what you have in front of you. Many influencers today talk about how you are in dire need to be an entrepreneur otherwise you would stay mediocre throughout your life. Other people want to be entrepreneurs because they want to be the in charge of their own time. Employees consider it better to be secure, getting their paycheck every two weeks and schedule their time, and the list goes on, there are thousands of conflicting opinions over this topic.

That is why I have had the opportunity to interview many entrepreneurs and employees about this wonderful debate, something that each one defends based on their facts.

"Un Café para Emprender" determined in their research that 78% of people argue that being an entrepreneur is the best, since it gives you more freedom in terms of time and finances, however, they have not been entrepreneurs, "they are employees". Similarly, 14% believe that it is best to be secure in a permanent job that can provide what is necessary to live according to their comforts, "those are not entrepreneurs as well", the remaining 8% says that entrepreneurship is not for everyone, only the bold people with certain capabilities and mindset should go on this venture, those have undertaken the risk and are entrepreneurs.

In the end, these are statistics extracted from a group of people. It is not the absolute truth, but it can help us predict certain behavior of the people.

Whatever your choice is or whatever path you take, it would be good only if you develop it and exploit it in the best way, or else it would turn to be bad depending on the choices you make along the way.

In this book we not only have combined the experience of employees, entrepreneurs or big businessmen, but also the experience of the people who complement these experimenters in the world of work.

Let's enter the rational economic brain of people and get to know the benefits of being an entrepreneur, an employee or both at the same time, advantages and disadvantages, costs and income along with their economic aspect.

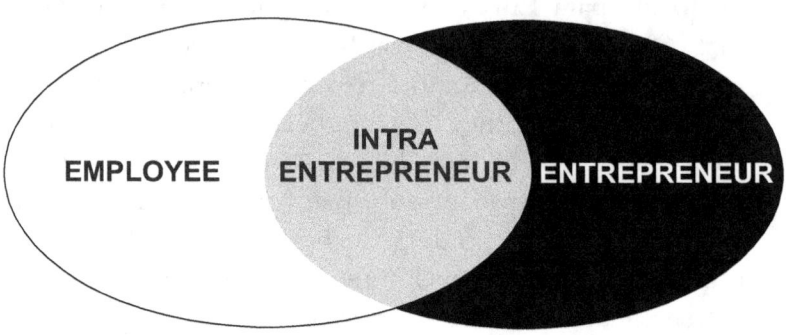

You can be an Employee, an Intra-entrepreneur or an Entrepreneur who in time can become a great businessman.

Being an Employee

Being an Employee "EmpleaT"

"EmpleaT = Get Employed = Being an Employee."

A lot of people have stigmatized being an employee. In this era, to be an employee is to be a slave of a company having a specific schedule "Time in with no time out", an adequate compensation at a rate agreed upon by the business economic regime.

All this has distorted the nature of the employee, as well as its value in an organization.

While it is true that an employee is bounded by clauses stipulated in a contract, it does not mean that he cannot surpass the limits imposed on his growth and potential and/or cannot aspire to be at very high levels in an organization where he can obtain financial freedom or wealth.

In today's world there are many employees with excellent positions and incredible salaries that exceed what more than 80% of the companies in the world earn. Such is the case of the CEO of the technology conglomerate Alphabet "Google Corporate" with a basic salary of $2 million per year plus compensation and the possibility of earning $240 million based on goals and targets achieved, this is a clear example that there is a possibility to be a multi-million dollar employee.

Being an employee

An employee is a person who provides his or her time, expertise and services by performing a job in exchange for a salary from an employer or company.

A contract is formally created to validate the scope, responsibilities and benefits of the work to be performed and to protect the parties involved i.e. employee and employer.

An employee is the most valuable resource of a company and is the main engine to produce a product or service that provides value to that company, therefore, companies must implement policies for taking care of their most valuable resource.

Experience: I have been employed since I was 15 years old in different places. My first job was in a maquila plant of sardine cans and my first salary was $112.00 MXP per week, which for a boy of that age was a lot of money. Later at the age of 16, I worked as a waiter in a discotheque at 16, of course it was not legal to hire a boy of that age. Then after months of practice I worked as a substitute DJ, until I was the main DJ for at least 4 years. I also worked as a bricklayer, I cooked hamburgers and fried chicken, then a computer teacher, graphic designer, software developer and so I followed my professional path that led me to what I am now. In all those years I learned that my work was fundamental for the growth of each of the companies I worked for. The knowledge I applied in these companies helped stand out, making me a different kind of worker. Although the offered salary was fair, it was not enough for my needs that were to be fulfilled at that particular stage of life.

Having a job is a blessing that we should be grateful for every day. To give the best of ourselves because there is a company that gives us not only the opportunity to apply our knowledge, but also the opportunity to put food on the table. Many people complain about the job they have, the salary they are given or the duties they perform for their employer.

> "Never complain, never explain" If you are not satisfied with the situation, do something about it.
>
> *Henry Ford*

Being a great employee

All of us who have been employees, have at one time or another wished to be **great employees**.

Anyone can be an employee of a company; however, not just anyone can be **a great employee**. For that you must have qualities and capabilities greater than the average employee.

Some special characteristics that a great employee has are:

- Passion
  Employees who work with passion maintain a state of persistent desire involving the combination of rational and emotional thinking which shines through their work.
  It is very noticeable when an employee with passion is able to achieve result that is greater than expected because he not only fulfills the request but also adds a special touch.

- Communication
  A great employee is a great communicator of his ideas in the work environment. He stands out with the clarity of his messages that he wants to communicate and sends it through some channel (voice, written message, body language, etc.) where the receiver is able to decode that message and will be able to respond correctly.
  Effective communication makes you stand out from the rest of the team and adds value, visibility and trust. Although many communicators are born

with this quality, it can also be developed through the four basic language skills: speaking, listening, reading and writing.

- Teamwork
It is the ability to find the exact place in a work group where you can complement, cooperate, develop and enhance the capabilities of others in an organized manner within your team.
This characteristic makes a great employee, fostering a sense of loyalty, security and self-esteem to meet the individual needs of each member of the group, values belonging and fosters positive relationships in the organization or outside it.

- Commitment
It is the rational and emotional involvement of the employee with the company when he traverses through the challenges, projects and opportunities.
This characteristic is essential to achieve business success.
However, engaging employees is the responsibility of the company and it is here where the companies should pay full attention and find those employees who have a naturally higher level of engagement and empower them.
An engaged employee is empowered, proposes his own goals and directs his professional career within the framework of the company, takes risks, has an

enthusiasm for change and has a spirit of collaboration and teamwork.

- Proactive

A proactive employee is a key element in a company since he has a natural vision to detect a problem before others, propose a solution, execute it and show the result before it happens.

A proactive employee is of great value to the company. They are highly motivated employees capable of solving problems by proposing innovative and efficient solutions even for the most challenging problems.

- Attitude

This characteristic is one of the most significant characteristic of a good employee, since a good attitude has a great impact wherever you are.

A positive attitude drives us to seek information and solutions in the face of adversity and uncertainty of the future. In the fear of knowing the answer to our doubts, we often get blocked by our emotions; this is what prevents us from adopting positive attitudes.

It is understandable that it is not easy to have a positive attitude all the time, however, it is something that certain people know how to manage very well.

The energy that is emanated by the attitude you have can worsen or improve the environment of an area, a work team or an office in particular.

> "A bad attitude is like a flat tire, you can't go anywhere until you change it.
>
> *Unknown*

In addition to having some outstandingly good peculiar characteristics, it is inevitable to mention that a great employee is always available to help his colleagues, takes things very seriously and tries to finish his tasks faster than anyone else, he also sacrifices his time to ace the assigned tasks. He becomes exceptionally good, making difficult things look easy. He gains the trust of his colleagues and his essence is noticed in the workplace. He adapts to any environment no matter how difficult it may be and is the first to sacrifice his interests to keep the adverse situation under control, seeking ultimate success.

A great employee has same intellectual and physical capabilities like a common employee, but with a big difference over others, "Always with a great ATTITUDE".

He has his eyes fixed on the prize i.e. the result. He does not seek gratitude instead he strives for respect. He does not complain about problems, he looks for solutions. He knows that the process is painful, but he knows that it is temporary. He feels the excitement of belonging to a team where he can show his skills and experience. He is willing to learn and apply his knowledge along the way. He takes off with one goal at a time and goes for it.

Anyone can be a great employee, but not everyone wants to pay the price that comes with it.

> "If you can't or won't pay the price to be extraordinary, don't complain about being ordinary.
>
> *Humberto Aguilar*

Experience: In one of my jobs I was fortunate to have a boss a couple of years younger than me. He was a general manager and I was a systems manager. At first I thought something was wrong because he looked ordinary by his apparent ways, just like everyone else. I decided to observe him to understand why he was my boss and not the other way around. I realized that he was a very well prepared guy; he knew his duties perfectly, had an unmatched commanding voice and was very level-headed. In the meetings with the owners of the company I observed that he was always very practical, very confident, he had clear and forceful answers. One day I asked him how he did it and he told me, it's like soccer, just because you are right foot player, doesn't mean you can't touch the ball with your left foot, you can also use your head, shoulder, back and everything else. You have to do more than others, put some extra efforts and spend more time than others to achieve what they will never achieve.

Meritocracy

One of the most complicated challenges to understand is meritocracy.

Meritocracy (a term from the Latin merĭtum 'due reward', in turn from mereri 'to earn, deserve'; and the suffix -cracia from the Greek krátos, or κράτος in Greek, 'power, strength') or rule of the best is a form of government based on merit.

Meritocracy **exists only in the dictionary**, since inequality and injustice in the labor and institutional order has been disappearing year by year and the reality is that today it is more important to belong to a labor society **"labor sociocracy"** than to allow someone with greater capacity **"intelligence, studies, or greater preparation"** to join that closed and jealously guarded labor social group.

Nowadays, trying to move up is much more complex than expected, you have to belong to that social circle where the position you want is protected, create working relationships for convenience and networking, make daily bows to the bosses and maintain a submissive low-key profile before the authorities, at the end of all comes the merit if necessary.

What is the point of preparing so much?

Actually, preparation is important to increase meritocracy and reduce labor sociocracy. However, preparation must be well focused and aligned, so that it can permeate and align within the organizational structures, it is necessary in order to balance the jobs in an organizational structure with the studies, experience, results and effort of an individual who is part of an organization.

Meritocracy is a socially structured proposal according to which, job positions are reserved for people who have training and experience that has been generated throughout their career. It is based on filling positions with the most qualified people and not by selection through friendship or patronage.

Sociocracy on the other hand was well designed earlier, but nowadays it lacks merit; anyone who is socially connected and networks well can aspire to a higher and faster position.

This has led us to study human behavior from another perspective "Neuroscience".

Neuroscience indicates that for the human being is more important:

1. His security
2. Belonging to a society
3. Truth

This means that meritocracy is part of truth; however, sociocracy is more important because it is part of belonging to a society.

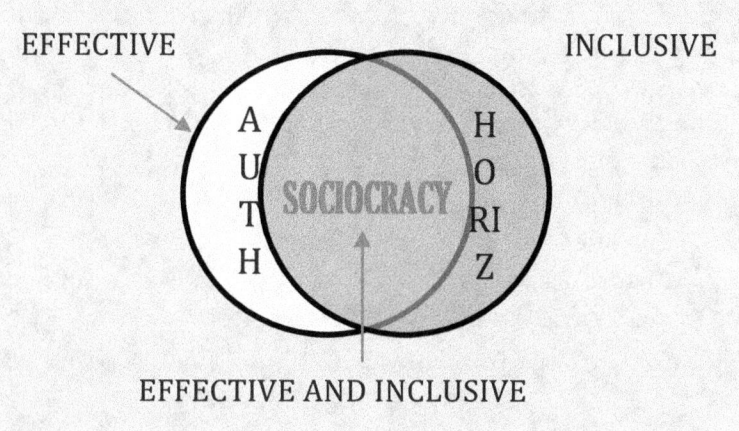

Sociocracy offers consent, groups the tasks and authority into roles, roles into teams which have been connected to keep everything aligned and transparent. However, sociocracy that is not controlled lacks merit, which makes everything move by convenience.

Basically, a person's IQ, titles and specializations are no longer important; the most important thing is empathy with the labor society and obedience.

Experience: Meritocracy has now become a social game with new rules rather than a merit game. I have seen how brilliant people with great work ethics have not climbed higher positions for the simple fact that they are not liked by their superiors or do not fit in their work social circle. It is indeed sad how people with zero talents and no commitment take positions that do not correspond to them, just for being a friend of the boss or recommended by friends of the boss, all thanks to reference and links.

I have seen a very few people, who by their own merit have managed to stand out in their jobs.

How to climb the ladder quickly

It is said that to climb the ladder quickly you must be good at what you do, meet your established schedules, have a college degree, preferably a master's degree, make merit and have a good reputation.

As per the reality check this is a total lie. To climb the ladder quickly you must know how to play the game of the work society in which you are developing. Understand who is at the head of the organization and see what kind of people surround them, learn from each of their positions and start with a well-designed socialization program.

You have to study and understand well enough that who is your boss and the relationships he has with everyone around him.

> "Whoever leans close to a good tree is blanketed by a good shade.
>
> ***Miguel de Cervantes***

It is also essential to know which projects are more relevant to the organization and which projects are less relevant to your supervisors, to focus your efforts on the prioritized tasks and not waste time on projects that will not make you shine bright among your colleagues.

Best of all, you need to know how you should present your projects to your superiors. This is very important, since you make their work easier and they will not spend time on it and you will always be the one to present it to the managers, which will give you visibility and confidence.

In addition to all this, you should socialize outside the office to create closer bonds of acquaintance that will help you keep your supervisors anesthetized when you make mistakes.

This is the shortest way to move up the ladder quickly.

NOTE: The one thing you must not do is denigrate yourself, allow yourself to be disrespected or give up your honor to move up.

Experience: I have only found two ways to climb the ladder quickly:

Changing jobs, I have always been fortunate enough to be called by other companies on the recommendation of someone who works with me or knows my work; this has helped me move up the ladder fast than other people.

Aligning with the right supervisors, I had the opportunity to observe the supervisors who had the best relationships with their managers and what I did was to help them cover their commitments and objectives in such a way that they themselves recommended me and assigned me better projects to have greater visibility with the managers, which reflected in salary increment and job changes.

These are not the only two ways, however, these are the two that I have experienced and I believe are the least invasive.

Why don't GURUS climb the ladder?

Before going into detail on the subject matter, it is important to determine who is a GURU?

In Hinduism, guru means 'spiritual master'.

In a company, a GURU is a person who is an expert in his area and is respected for his knowledge, experience and ability to solve problems. However, these experts become so indispensable in their area that they are hardly promoted, as it is very difficult to replace them with someone equally or more capable. In addition, most GURUS are introverted, serious people who do not like to socialize and network openly with everyone around.

Organizations should have a social training program for employees of this type.

Despite being bright, committed and with above-average skills, most of them lack the social skills "also called soft skills" that are indispensable to bring them up to the next level. Companies prefer to put someone as a supervisor with social and managerial skills to control the GURUS, instead of investing time in training GURUS to socialize and network effectively.

Experience: I always wanted to be the best, the most knowledgeable, the one who solved all the problems, the person who could finish difficult projects, the one recognized by co-workers as the most capable, intelligent, wise, and indispensable in the organization. However, over time you realize that this also dampens your growth. I worked in a company for several years in a great position, but I could no longer aspire to a higher position because I was so proficient in my area that it was very difficult for my boss to get someone who was as committed as I was in my area of expertise. One day I asked him why he didn't help me to move up to a more administrative and less technical position. He told me, who is going to fill your place, who is going to do what you do, for that I will have to hire at least 3 people and train you in administrative matters as well. You are too important to be removed from where you are now.

Time to change jobs

Everything in life has an expiration period, nothing lasts forever.

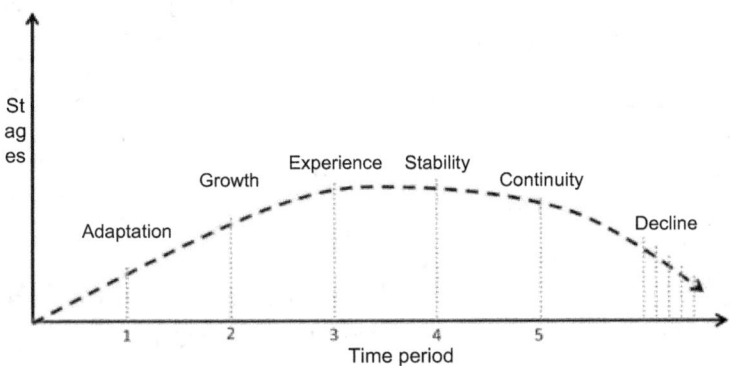

In jobs it is the same, there is a natural period of adaptation, growth, experience, stability, continuity and decline. These can be months or years depending on the nature of the job and how it develops.

There are many studies covering the subject matter that how long an employee should stay in a company and the timeline varies between 3 and 5 years. These studies fail to agree on the precision. However, 5 years is the most prominent period that an employee should stay in a company and some of their justifications are:

- Job stability
- Benefits

- Secure retirement
- Experience in a sector
- Enough to know and be an expert in the company.

However, so much depends on the country, culture, age, socioeconomic status and education.

If you ask a Japanese person about the subject matter, he will immediately answer that he wants to retire in the same organization i.e. all his working life.

If you ask an American, he will answer 3.5 to 5 years.

In addition, another factor is age, a 20 to 30 year old entry level employee is sure to answer 1 to 3 years and change to move up the ranks and increase his financial benefits. An average employee 31 to 40 year old will say 5 to 10 years and an employee over 40 will say more than 10 years until retirement.

Survey conducted by "Un café para Emprender"

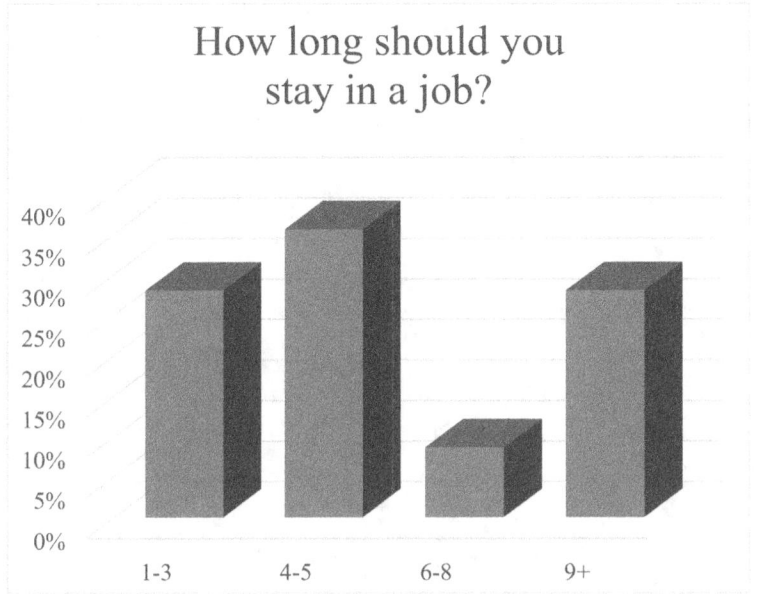

What is clear is that most employees have an average of 5 years to get to know the company, their position and their functions completely. If after that there are no major challenges to grow in your workplace, then it is time to migrate to new job adventures or entrepreneurship.

Experience: When I was young I changed jobs every year or every 2 years, which led me to understand that I was only doing it for a better salary and not for more experience. I knew that I lacked to develop more professionally, but I had the advantage of youth which is somehow permissible. Over time I tried to last longer and gained more experience, but it got to the point where the position was no longer interesting, there were no work related challenges to help me grow and no better salary up-scaling to cater my ever changing financial dynamics. I stayed in a job for 9 years which gave me great satisfaction, many challenges, I was very motivated, but a time came where the monotony of day to day chores took over me, I became particularly different, the chair was molded to my body, my intellectual horizon began to shrink and I stopped looking for subjects that made me grow. I had a stable job, good salary, but I had no challenges and that led me to seek new opportunities in other companies and creating my own ventures.

How to take care of your employees so they don't leave

One of the most important needs a company has is to keep its employees motivated and that too with the conviction to stay with the company for a longer period of time.

But why do employees leave? "Un Café para Emprender" tells us:

WHY LEAVE YOUR CURRENT JOB?

- Seeking new opportunities
- Balance Work/life
- Excessive Stress
- Lack of motivation

Sell them the mission and vision of the company and make them feel safe, reliable and necessary all the time, but not indispensable.

The first thing we must understand is that nothing and no one is indispensable in a company, therefore, a business is not based on feelings at first place, it should be treated as people who provide a service in the company and are in turn rewarded with a salary.

This does not mean that you do not have personal appreciation and/or share time and moments with your employees. What it does mean is that in business there are no feelings; feelings are in people, unless your employees are family members where there is an additional bond.

Experience: Each employee of a company should be valued based on the activities, achievements and objectives assigned and achieved by him. There are some qualities that the employee must have to fulfill its tasks. If for some reason he does not meet those qualities, he must be trained. In every company I worked in, I tried to find the right courses for my work team, in order to increase their capabilities and skills, upgrade their knowledge, reduce risks and increase productivity. Many people told me "don't invest in them, they will leave" and I found two types of people, those who leave after preparing them "20%" and those who stay grateful for having received "80%" training.

Competitive employees

In every company there are employees who are very competitive and stand out from the rest because their competitive drive is so great and stands out in such a way that it can be perceived within the organization.

These competitive employees seek immediate recognition and are to be placed on the important positions within the organization. Mostly this does not happen because the culture of the company does not provide for it. This causes the most competitive employees to become discouraged and look for better options in the market.

Many of those competitive employees become discouraged for different reasons:

- There is no healthy competition
- They are constrained by their supervisors
- They are sabotaged by envious coworkers
- Their salary is not congruent with the value they provide to the organization
- Lack of motivation
- Lack of training
- Excessive stress
- They do not have a defined career plan

Training

There are a few things in this world that are a lifetime investment; this stance is particularly true with training, as they say "the best investment a person can make is in their knowledge".

In the same context, the best investment a person can make is in their own education. It does not bring immediate benefits, but does generate a strong impact on the overall outlook of the person in the long run.

> "Education is a long-term investment with intermediate benefits.
>
> ***Humberto Aguilar***

Many companies are afraid to educate their employees because once they are trained they leave for better economic benefits, this is very common particularly in tech based areas. However, it is necessary to continuously train employees for better performance and quality in the product and / or service to be performed.

Skills that an employee should be trained in:

- Social skills or soft skills. Based on personal relationships, this is one of the areas that should be covered but unfortunately is the one that receives the least attention.
  This skill can help strengthen and refine skills such as teamwork, leadership and honesty.
- Technical Skills

This is the solely focused skill in terms of training in most of the companies, since it is of utmost importance for the product or service to be of high quality and trustworthy.

- Teamwork

  Unity is strength and this skill is responsible for the creation and management of excellent work groups.

- Communication skills

  Every employee should be able to communicate in an effective way which is comprehend-able for all.

  Nowadays, we are looking for people capable of observing, listening and understanding a conversation, as well as processing and transmitting a message fluently and assertively.

- Leadership

  This ability has the characteristic of creating solid work groups, executing projects in a timely manner, and influencing people to work enthusiastically for a common goal.

  A leader stands out from the crowd by his ability to make the right decisions for the group, team or organization.

- Honesty and integrity

  Honesty is the way of acting in a real way, behaving with loyalty, compassion and sincerity; it is a very desirable quality in organizations indeed.

  Integrity is to act in a correct and congruent manner. A quality that is remarkable and sociably accepted.

- Personal finances
    This skill is one of the most overlooked and of utmost importance for employees to have.
    A financially well managed employee is a happy employee; he has no financial woes because he knows how to manage himself correctly.
    This ability allows employees to be economically stable and well informed about their financial matters, since bad personal finances is a distraction for the employee in his work environment and propitious to make big mistakes.

Experience: There are few companies that care about developing their employees in different areas of personal and professional growth. It is true that everything has a cost and training is no exception. However, training key employees will be an investment in the medium and long term. Companies such as AT&T, General Electric, Google, etc. have a budget allocated to this type of training.

No one is indispensable

In a company, no one is indispensable and anyone who thinks so is making a fool out of himself.

We have been educated by society and our parents that we must keep our positions by learning everything about the position and being the best of all in order to become indispensable.

History tells us that people who become indispensable do not get promoted; on the contrary, they stagnate like still water and are just like the hamster on the wheel, going round and round all the time without advancing anywhere.

These people stay in the same job for years, they become specialists and valuable for their ability to solve problems, however, they only generate value in that sector, but are not able to generate value in positions where resources must be managed.

Therefore, if you believe that becoming indispensable in a company is what will lead you to permanence for many years, then it may be possible, but if you believe that being indispensable will lead you to climb important positions in the organization, I am sorry to tell you are undoubtedly very wrong.

There is no fix or designated time at which you have zero chances of advancing in your career, you only need to amp up your game by upgrading and polishing your social and networking skills to be able to complement and seek a higher position.

A company does not have feelings of empathy and sympathy so at any moment it can replace an employee with another one, no matter how valuable the previous one may seem. Sometimes it prefer to pay the price of getting someone else than to keep the same employee.

An employee who thinks that he is indispensable is not a GURU, but he has certain problem solving characteristics and skills.

Experience: in all the companies I have known there is at least one employee who thinks he is indispensable, to such an extent, that this person is arrogant, and thinks he has rights over others since he knows the most about certain tasks and channels of the company. Most of the employees around him submit to that employee since they know he is the most experienced and no one wants to spend time learning what that employee knows and prefer him to solve the issues. However, it becomes uncomfortable and even slows down the pace of the project at times.

> "The one who helps the most is more indispensable than the one who knows the most.
>
> *Humberto Aguilar*

Degrees and qualifications do not make good employees

For decades we have been educated, not to say deceived, we have been sold this false narrative that we must pursue a college degree because it differentiates a good employee from a mediocre one. It is a fallacy very well designed by organizations and governments, which our parents have blindly bought and passed on to us.

Although that line of having a degree to aspire a well-paid job is rapidly dissipating, although there are a few jobs that strictly necessitate the need to have a degree, would you allow a surgeon to operate on your heart without having a degree?

Jobs used to be divided into specialized and professional jobs.

- Specialized
  For these types of jobs, a college degree is not necessary, as only one of two things was required:
  1. Years of experience
     Experience is one of the most important characteristics so it is graded in terms of beginner, intermediate or expert.
     Example: intermediate welder with 3 years of experience.
  2. Certification
     A certification is only a document endorsed by an educational institution specialized in attesting and legalizing that you have

passed the skills test concerning a specific subject.
Example: Installer of alarm systems in buildings.
- Professionals
In this type of jobs it is strictly necessary to graduate from a university where the study program is 100% accredited, as well as to graduate in order to prove the specialization to the hiring companies, guaranteeing the acquisition of apt knowledge which may suffice for a particular job or position.

However, today it is indispensable to have a degree but it is not necessary.

Many companies, mostly tech based companies "like Google, Amazon and Tesla" employ people for their experience, expertise and specialty, rather than for their professional degree.

It is well proven in certain cases that degrees do not solely make good employees. There are employees who are more prepared, committed and have years of experience than professionals with degrees in the job market.

Why do employees resign?

In companies or institutions most of the times, managers do not realize why their staff resigns. However, in the world there are many statistics and strong research that provide data relevant to our topic, depending on the country.

Most of these statistics agree that 90% of the employees resign because of their supervisor's ill treatment.

It is important to note that this type of resignation also has its positive side since 15% of the employees who resign become entrepreneurs building their own companies, which generates jobs.

> "Every bad side has a good side, even if it is not of the same proportion.
> ***Humberto Aguilar***

Employee myths

There are many employee myths that need to be uncovered. Things nowadays are not like they used to be in the past and technology has helped to change the rules of the game, just as the COVID 19 pandemic had its great impact.

Here are some of the most outstanding employee myths:

- Age is no longer a factor
  Decades ago, employees used to fret over their working age because of some invisible limits that companies required to hire staff. A technology person in their 40s was considered a veteran and their hiring opportunities diminished considerably. This forced them to start or change careers. Or contrary to this, it also caused them to stay with the same company for years until they retired because they thought they would not be hired elsewhere because of the age factor.
  Since the technological boom age has taken a back seat, it is no longer a factor to be considered in many professional jobs. Now experience has more professional value than age.
- Gender equality
  In first world countries gender discrimination has almost disappeared to a great extent and equality is noticeable in many sectors since the law has taken a participatory role in the control of discrimination. Today women are competing strongly in the top positions of large organizations, to mention a few:

Karen Lynch, CEO of CVS Health, Jane Fraser, CEO, Citi, Julie Sweet, president and CEO, Accenture, Carol Tomé, CEO, UPS and Mary Barra, president and CEO of GM. Similarly, the LGBT+ community has great leaders such as: Tim Cook, CEO, Apple, Jim Fitterling, CEO, Dow Chemical Company, Jeffrey Gennette, CEO, Macy's, Beth Ford, CEO, Land O'Lakes and Anne Richards, CEO, Fidelity International to name a few.

In third world countries gender discrimination has been much worse and complicated; however, they have come a long way in terms of equality.

- The condition

Fortunately, technology has a good and powerful side that has allowed us to employ people who are differently able, who can performed in specific areas of their expertise.

Businessmen and entrepreneurs have been crucial in this inclusion and have obtained not only a great employee, but also, great economic benefits from the different governments, depending on each country.

- Geography

Now it is possible to work from home "Home Office" or from any place we want because companies have realized that the results are more important for the company than the place where you work, plus the new trend called work from home allows companies to save a significant amount of money on office expenses such as bills and maintenance, etc.. Not all jobs are fortunate to work from home or from some other place remotely as a plumber, waiter, welder, etc.

> "Myths which are believed in tend to become true.
>
> *George Orwell*

Does being an employee give you financial freedom?

To begin with, we must understand what financial freedom is, and to this day there is no single agreed-upon definition on the subject matter. Each person is responsible for his or her definition of financial freedom; however, the current proposed definitions have some arguments in common.

Financial freedom as a term has been very popular in the United States at the beginning of the century by authors such as Robert Kiyosaki or the precursors of the FIRE movement "Financial Independence, Retire Early".

As a generic concept, financial freedom is the ability of a person to earn a certain income that can cover his or her financial expenses by doing what he likes to do or by doing nothing at all.

According to this concept, if an employee can achieve financial freedom based on his salary, "he can do a lot depending on his position, competencies, commitments, management of his finances and diversification".

There are many employees in the world who have achieved financial freedom and can stop working and continue living comfortably anytime.

> "Wealth consists not in having great possessions, but in having few wants.
>
> ***Epicteto***

Experience: As an employee you can achieve financial freedom if you are able to manage your finances in an organized manner, where your expenses do not exceed your budgets and using part of your income in medium and long term investments, in addition to paying debts and passive commitments.

It may not be easy; however, it is not impossible. It is similar to desiring a perfect body but you have to make sacrifices and have perseverance to achieve it.

The important thing is that, it is possible to have financial freedom by being an employee in a company.

Take a Risk

ArriesgaT (Take Risk)

It is easy to invite others to take risks and do something but those who incite others are not willing to take the crucial step and this is very common in all times.

If you want to achieve something you would always have to pay its price, however, you do not always know what the price to be paid is and that is where you must take your own risks.

To take risks is to control your fears, establishing clear objectives of your ultimate destination where you are headed, and look inside yourself for the necessary tools and motivational drive to do it. No one says it's easy, because if it were, anyone would do it.

> "Since you are a novice in terms of worldly matters, all the things that seem difficult from the outside seem impossible to you... Trust in time that usually provides sweet solutions to many bitter difficulties
>
> *Don Quixote*

The greater the risk, the greater is the reward, and the greater the knowledge, the lesser the risk or measured risk, thus increasing the probability of obtaining the greatest reward.

It seems like a maze, but the secret is in preparation, experience and resilience. This is the point where your risk makes sense and its nuance begins to show.

That's why when someone tells you "ArriesgaT" (Take risk) it's because they see the preparation in you; they've noticed your talent and know your experience and outlook. But you need to sit down, think about the next step to work on and evaluate the available tools you have to take the leap.

Experience: I have taken many risks in both of my careers i.e. as an employee and as an entrepreneur. These risks have had mixed results sometimes I lost and sometimes I won. No one has given me anything for free and I am convinced that sometimes you have to take the risk and learn the hard way.

One day I was told at my job to go to Houston to develop a system and that I would be traveling 2 weeks in the USA, 4 weeks in Mexico. My English was very poor and I remembered that a teacher advised us to put more interest in English than in any other subject. The truth is that I repeatedly insulted myself for not taking the advice seriously as I used to escape English lessons and treated them as play time.

I decided to take the risk of accepting that project. Once I took it I regretted every day, but I set out to learn the language quickly, at least technically to be able to express myself. I was fortunate to bring the project to good terms with my language limitations.

To this day I take a lot of risks because I know my skills and I know I can do it.

Is a college degree necessary?

A college degree does not make an employee or an entrepreneur, a college degree is only a document that certifies that a person managed to successfully complete the assignments of a study program related to a career, which is required in the labor market.

A college degree is important because guarantees the value of a person's knowledge.

While it is true that a college degree is very important, it is also true that it is not for all types of jobs and this is where the confusion begins, the way big companies of the world are hiring their employees.

Companies like Google, Amazon and Microsoft have revolutionized the way they hire technical staff, but their criteria cannot be generalized. To hire a developer does not require a university degree, but it does require experience and the evaluation is different, it can be through an exam or through a certification "this plays a big role in the equation", on the contrary to hire a doctor it does require a university degree, as well as his credentials matter and does not accept doctors who do not have the degree, besides that by law any mistake can prove to be fatal.

"Would you be willing to undergo a brain surgery by a person who does not have a degree to back it up?"

This way of hiring has become very popular in American companies especially for the tech base jobs because of the shortage of skilled employees. That's why it's much faster and convenient to groom a person in a two-week to one-month specialization than to wait for them to finish a college degree.

> "A college degree says little, but the security that comes from having learned a skill says everything
>
> *Unknown*

Experience: Always with my eagerness to be the best among all, I sought to obtain a university degree, a master's degree, certifications and everything necessary to be recognized as a great professional.

I have had many disappointments when I headed on this path and I am not saying that it is bad to have a degree, on the contrary, it is very good to have a document that supports what you have studied and learned.

In all the companies I have worked for, the first 2 asked me for a copy of my degree just to fulfill the requirement. The rest of the companies never asked me for any document as proof of my studies what I put in my resume, only the US government asked me for my certified school documents when I went forward to obtain residency.

Traveling

Before you make the decision to jump on the bandwagon of entrepreneurship, it is important to take into account what successful people recommend: traveling, traveling, traveling...

As an employee and/or entrepreneur, traveling will open a new world to you, it is same as changing frequency and adapting a better, wider outlook with more possibilities to grow.

Traveling expands the mind, increases creativity, improves health, strengthens relationships, helps to socialize, produces happiness and improves mood.

According to Shimi Kang, a doctor in the neuroscience of happiness and health, giving the brain some downtime helps restore it. And what is a better way to escape the monotony of this mundane life than to go on a trip?

Traveling gives you many benefits such as:

- Increased self-confidence
- Broader geographical knowledge
- Helps you get to know and recognize yourself
- Opens your mind to other cultures and people
- You learn to make mistakes and pick yourself up again

> "It's easy to be brave when you have nothing to lose
>
> **_Unknown_**

Working in Germany, England, France, Hungary, El Salvador, Mexico, the United States or any other country is not the same as the rest of the world, that's why traveling opens the mind and shows what's wonderful about each culture.

When a company is recruiting new employees, the first thing they look for is that if they have traveled, that if they have a diverse cultural background and that the employee understands how other countries work. It doesn't matter if you have a master's degree, a doctorate or thousands of awards.

Experience: One day my boss comes to me saying, please support a colleague. You are going to Bremen, Germany to the satellite company OHB https://www.ohb.de/en/ and take the next project for them to build a device that we need. I accept that I was very scared at that time, I had to travel alone, I did not know how to speak German, I was not fluent in English either. But this trip changed my outlook of the world, my brain became more receptive and I learned that there were different cultures than mine, different laws, climate, clothes, food, etc. Since then I have been to more than 30 countries and I have been able to interpret the way others think depending on their country.

Choosing the right people

It may sound cliché, but it is a reality, to this day I have not read any book on entrepreneurship that touches this important topic.

Don't believe everything people say. Many, if not most people who know you or are related to you, will not buy your product or service; they might even criticize you for what you do. It is important to take the position of the praying mantis that is deaf and uses the camouflage of nature, in order to avoid being manipulated by the opinions of people who do not contribute anything positive towards your journey.

Do not rely on empty phrases and shallow words that do not contribute anything. Whoever is going to help you grow will join your venture with knowledge, money, contacts or skills that can make your business grow.

Negative people around you drain your soul and encapsulate you in their world of fantasies, envy, mental poverty, misguided advice, malicious messages and they always give you camouflage advice that seems very accurate apparently but can actually lead you astray from your true path.

> "Nothing is as dangerous as good advice accompanied by bad example.
>
> *Madame de Maintenon*

Experience: One day I had a great idea, which I wanted to develop and I was very confident that it could be a great venture. I went to some friends with much more experience than me and told them individually about my project, one told me that it already existed in the market, that I should not invest time in it, another told me not to invest time in it because it was very difficult to reach the target market, etc., I let myself be carried away by all the bad comments and misleading advice and I was convinced that it was a bad idea. After 3 years, someone else made that idea a reality and today it is a successful company.

Protect your essence, but don't repress it

A typical mistake that most people make in their jobs as well as in their endeavors is to repress their essence so that they may save themselves from being the victims of the environment.

The mistake of hiding or repressing the natural essence of who we are is very common.

Just as each person has a physical imprint that distinguishes his personality from others, he also has his essence that is untouchable, but that essence is distinguishable and makes his presence felt in every place where he stays.

Sometimes we hear people laugh and we know who made them laugh, sometimes we distinguish someone by the simple fact of how the environment changes by the impact that their essence produces. When you go to work you realize that the boss has arrived by the behavior of the co-workers as they change their behavior and body language that has nothing to do with the beauty or appearance of the boss, it has to do with their essence, it is what imposes and gives strength to their inner self in some special way.

The essence is the heart of the self, of the ego, of the inner strength of every individual on this earth. Essence creates a significant difference between two people with the same complexion, age, height and beauty. It distinguishes one from the other, even if they look like two drops of water. Essence is what will make people respect, love, and desire or follow a person.

The essence must be protected, but never repressed, much less hidden, because hiding it hides the true person inside.

The essence is what makes the difference between a good employee and a mediocre one. It creates a difference between a successful entrepreneur and a mediocre entrepreneur. Essence makes a difference between a good person and a bad person.

Essence is your invisible interpretation without anyone having to see you and contains the hidden power of your distinction.

> "You don't need anyone to define or complete you; you come ready-made, with all your characteristics organized: it's called essence.

Walter Riso

Experience: I have always been an extrovert and a very cheerful person, which brought me many problems in the work environment since many people told me that I should be more serious and formal according to my position. After hearing the same message several times, I decided to change and started to develop myself according to the serious and formal profile I was "supposed" to be. A month later my boss invites me to lunch and asks me, what's wrong with you, do you have problems at home, is something wrong at work, have we done something to you that you don't like, etc. thousands of questions in such a short time. My answer was, everything is fine, nothing is wrong, I am alright. But my boss insisted and was very eager to know if there is something he could do to alleviate my situation so I decided to tell him. They were telling me to behave, to be more formal, more serious and that's what I am doing. He smiles and tells me; never stop being the way you are. No one will understand you. Whoever criticizes does so based on his own shortcomings. You are natural like that and don't lose your essence, so go back to being who you are.

Intra-entrepreneur

The term intra-entrepreneur is based on the designation of an employee who is capable of developing entrepreneurial outlook in terms of his performance by the way he plans and executes things and is widely supported by the company in which he works. He sets out for discovering new opportunities, evaluate them and take maximum advantage of them to create new businesses for the benefit of the company with which he collaborates.

In other words, an intra-entrepreneur is an employee who possesses the qualities and the support of his or her employers to undertake and assume entrepreneurship within the company.

> "There are lots of bad reasons to start a company. But there´s only one good, legitimate reason, and I think you know what it is: it´s to change the world.
>
> *Phil Libin*

There are some major differences between being an employee, intra-entrepreneur or entrepreneur.

	Employee	Intra Entrepreneur	Entrepreneur
Earnings	No	No	Yes
Salary	Fixed	Fixed	Variable
Schedule	8 hrs.	8 hrs.	24 hrs.
Bonus	No	Yes	No
Commission	Yes	Yes	No
Risk	Low	Medium	High
Training	Specialist	Specialist	Jack-of-all-trades

Experience: In my experience I have seen a very few people with such a high sense of responsibility and great vision who have been able to sell their unique ideas with unique selling points in the companies where they work, making agreements as intra-entrepreneurs where they have committed to receive a fixed salary, but with the condition of developing more business opportunities for their employers.

These intra-entrepreneurs obtain great rewards for their work and become the right arm of the owners of the company.

The leap from employee to entrepreneur

The greatest desire of an employee is to create his own company, manage his own time and earn a lot of money. Salary serves as shackles for an employee. Leaving a job is somehow tough, since the brain prefers the sense of security over anything else, the risk of losing what has been achieved so far keeps the employees from taking risks.

Although many employees are very well prepared professionally, even with myriad of achievements and years of experience behind them, they do not dare to take the next step.

Only 15% of entrepreneurs have important motives that push them to take the risk, such as:

- Financial independence
- To be their own boss
- Recognition
- Flexibility of schedule
- Learning
- Job creation
- Diversify income
- See opportunity in the same company they work for

> "Wonderful destinations usually have difficult roads
>
> ***Humberto Aguilar***

The reality is that most employees who have taken the leap into entrepreneurship have done so for reasons other than the entrepreneurial spirit. Among many reasons some of them are:

- Lack of employment
- They were fired
- They suffered a tragedy
- Mistreatment at the hands of their superior
- End of the project they were working on

Experience: My first entrepreneurship was when I was an employee of a company and I realized that it was very difficult to be an entrepreneur and work at the same time. When you have a fixed salary and you are starting a business, you still feel secure because you have the money to pay the bills; however, that same security makes you not to put 100% of your effort into the venture because there is no additional pressure other than the drive of the motivation to build your own business.

AdaptaT (Adaptation)

If anything in this world makes an employee or entrepreneur successful, it is adaptation.

Our world is made up of millions of people with different caliber consisting of different capabilities, character and conditions, who live in an environment that is constantly changing through the years.

The time of COVID 19 pandemic was the time that totally changed humanity and taught us the fragility of human life. It taught us that, in the face of any crisis we must change our business model to adapt to the current circumstances.

Unfortunately, people waste a lot of time trying to control everything around them so as not to feel fragile and waste a lot of resources that could be used in important projects related to entrepreneurship.

Adaptation does not allow us to go with the flow, adaptation means to modify some of the fibers of our being to develop in some peculiar characteristics which are different from the usual ones. Such as, when you live at the sea level and change the location to live in the mountains, body will receive less oxygen and will have to adapt to that situation. This also applies at work where you must adapt to solve the problems of the area, team or company. In entrepreneurship the adaptation is more complex and must be more ingenious to meet the needs of customers in a timely manner and to map out and execute projects successfully.

In itself, we are in constant changes that we must adapt quickly to be able to surf in them.

> "Intelligence is the ability to adapt to change.
>
> *Stephen Hawking*

Experience: One of my ventures called Mobile Business is dedicated to the creation of mobile workstations and creation of food trailers or food trucks in Houston, Texas, US. When I started this business I began by building the first professional makeup artist workstation with a new design. The problem was that it didn't sell immediately and the shop rent had to be paid, employee salaries and overhead expenses, plus my family and I had my own bills to pay too. We realized that the market also required welders who could do different types of projects and we had to take those projects as a cash flow alternative. We adapted the shop to do welding and painting additionally. With this we managed to keep the business running and were able to add new services to our product and service portfolio.

Learning entrepreneurship

In many ventures, the entrepreneur does not necessarily need to know how to create the product or service he is offering. Sometimes the entrepreneur sees an opportunity, gets the expert and solves the client's need. Fortunately, there are many entrepreneurs with these skills.

Entrepreneurship requires the understanding of many diverse concepts which are necessary for the venture to be successful.

It is important to have knowledge of several disciplines to be able to manage a venture and set it on the road to success.

According to an investigation by "Un Café para Emprender", the following recommendations were obtained from entrepreneurs and businessmen on this subject matter.

Respondents agreed that an entrepreneur should prepare himself/herself in the following areas:

1. Personal finances
   If you are able to manage your finances, it is highly liked that you will be able to start a business.
2. Sales and customer service
   It is essential to be able to take the product and/or service to the customer's door and follow up for getting the feedback to create a brand identity based on quality and good service.
3. Marketing

The exploration, creation and delivery of a product and/or service to satisfy the needs of the target market with effective marketing strategies.

4. Business Plan

   A business plan will help operate a business. It is a guide that will serve as a road map to structure, operate and grow the business maximizing profits and minimizing bleeding costs.

5. Innovation

   This is a great process that allows the introduction of novelties that improve the product and/or service offered.

> "The greatest enemy of knowledge is not ignorance; it is the illusion of knowledge.
>
> *Stephen Hawking*

Experience: I totally agree with the recommendations of the respondents. In my first ventures I failed to create and follow up on a business plan and for that reason it was very difficult for me to move forward. Although the idea was very good and it was clear to me what I wanted to do, there was a step-by-step follow-up plan so that no details could escape my eye.

I believe that an entrepreneur should not start a business if he does not have these 5 skills.

When should you quit your job?

As an employee there is a time when motivation is at rock bottom, the routine is heavy and mundane, coexistence is not pleasant and the environment is perceived monotonous from our perspective.

> "Your time is limited, so don't waste it living someone else's life. Don't be trapped by dogma, which is living with the results of other people´s thinking. Don't let the noise of others' opinions drown out your own inner voice. And most importantly, have the courage to follow your heart and your intuition. They somehow already know what you truly want to become. Everything else is secondary.
>
> ***Steve Jobs***

There are thousands of signs we must visualize before making a decision.

5 signs you should consider quitting your job

1. Doing the same thing for years
2. You can't aspire to be at better positions
3. When you are not happy with your current position
4. When monotony hits your creative window
5. When knowing that you have to go to work is unpleasant.

Before resigning you must prepare yourself to do it, not just make the decision and that's it. You must analyze and understand the situation. Try to leave the previous job while staying in the best terms with everyone around and look for a new place, establishing new objectives.

Experience: in my previous job I realized that I was already cycled, I felt wasted, like a hamster ready for any problem and there was no real motivation to keep me attentive to any project. My equation with some people had become unpleasant and I felt uneasy. My smile had faded and so had my desire to belong to this company that had given me so much. I didn't want to be rude or leave from one day to the next. I had an excellent relationship with the owner that I could not be bad with him so I had to communicate my position with him. At first, 2 years before, I told him that I wanted to start a business, that I no longer saw myself in the company, he told me to pursue a master's degree and that he would pay for it, to which I replied that I had one and I did not want any more. I let time pass and the next time I insisted, seeking his approval. He gave me the runaround, until one day I realized that he was prepared enough to let me go. He invited me to lunch and gave me the opportunity to leave the company on very good terms. We negotiated that I would stay 3 more months to cover for my absence and teach the person who would be in my place. I will be forever grateful to him for that and other gestures he made to me. To this day I am always attentive to any problem, doubt or inconvenience they have to help them solve.

Be an Entrepreneur

EmprendeT (Be an Entrepreneur)

When you are ready to be an entrepreneur?

Actually, you don't know it, it´s a feeling and that is the most powerful feeling that can push you to take the next life changing step.

There are many factors that can determine if you are ready to become an entrepreneur:

- A great idea
  Many of us have had great ideas and someone else materialized it. The most important thing about a great idea is that it facilitates authenticity and the possibility of doing something unique. However, a great idea is not enough if it is not carried out. We've all had great ideas, but we limit ourselves so much that we don't do anything.
- Vision
  It is the ability to see beyond what others see, where imagination is very powerful and creates surreal realities.
  It is the ideal expectation of what is expected from an employee or entrepreneur in the future. He should be realistic, practical and ambitious.
- Capital
  The exchangeable element between time and resources that gives life to the venture is capital. It is always necessary to have a capital of 6 to 9 months, which is the average time to know if your venture will be profitable or not.

- Preparation
  One of the factors that determine if you are ready to start a business is your homework about what you want to start. If you are going to start a restaurant it is important to have the necessary knowledge to be able to manage a restaurant.
- Previous experience in what you are going to undertake
  Experience is one of the most solid factors when it comes to entrepreneurship but it is not theoretical, it is practical and it takes time to become an expert in a business to facilitate the success of the venture itself.
- Talent
  Talent is the ability of a person to perform an activity, task or job with natural ability, and without effort.
  If you have a talent and you want to move ahead using your talent, you are on the right track.
- Motivation
  The inner motive that causes a person to take action is motivation. Motivation is born inside a person and ultimately reflects on the outside through action.
  Having a motivation for entrepreneurship is indispensable because it gives you the strength you need to take steps forward.
- Mentor
  Having a mentor is extremely essential for entrepreneurship since their experience will not

make you start from scratch, but from their experience and you will learn during the process.

Mentors are usually not free and you will have to pay for their time and expertise. It is worth having one because it helps to reduce the time for the venture to be successful.

- Work plan

    Before making the decision to start a business, it is of utmost importance to create a work plan which will serve to follow up the venture in an orderly fashion. As a personal advice extracted through my failures I recommend you NOT to start a business if you do not have a work plan.

However, these factors do not guarantee success, but they do help you get closer to your goal.

> "You have to trust in something, your gut, destiny, life, karma, whatever.
>
> *Steve Jobs*

Experience: these factors are important, however, the most important for me is having a mentor, that person who helps to make an idea a reality from his or her experience. The mentor always seeks to motivate the entrepreneur with practical teachings and always looking for the benefit of the entrepreneur. Professional mentors are not free and are costly sometimes, but they are very effective and worth the money, necessary for any entrepreneurship.

When is the best time to be an entrepreneur?

Entrepreneurship is not a game; it is not about registering a company to say that you are an entrepreneur. Entrepreneurship is an art and it requires a lot of courage, time, effort and follow-up.

Statistics are not favorable for entrepreneurs. In fact, statistics are always against entrepreneurs.

85% of ventures die in the first 3 years, 95% die before 10 years.

Based on this statistic, **when is the best time to become an entrepreneur?**

The best time is when the interest to become independent takes birth within a person. Although there is not an exact designated moment to start a business, a date, an age, there is only one reason, you have to be prepared to start a business.

The most important thing is to know what you want to undertake, to look for the necessary learning and to give shape to that idea that is waiting to be executed on a daily basis.

Know your talents and make the most of them.

> "There is only one way to avoid criticism: do nothing, say nothing and be nothing.

Aristotle

Experience: I started my first venture when I was 30 years old and I developed an ecommerce platform. It was my first failure and was indeed very painful. I got discouraged and didn't dare to start up again until 5 years later.

I pursued several ventures that failed, but they taught me that I was on the right path, as I was acquiring many skills needed for my next venture.

Today some of my ventures have matured, some of them are in the process of maturing and other ventures are in the incubator waiting for the time to capitalize and ignite them.

When should you NOT start a venture?

In the world of entrepreneurship there are many factors that must be taken into consideration before undertaking, but there are also factors that are indicative for you not to undertake a venture, such as:

- When an idea is not backed up by research
  It is normal that when we have an illusion, we seek to make it a reality and we trust that it will be a successful for the simple fact that our heart tells us "DO IT, IT WILL BE SUCCESSFUL". Investigate first if your illusion is feasible and viable enough to be turned into reality.
- When you are not willing to sacrifice more than 8 hours a day.
  Entrepreneurship does not mean that you will work less than an employee; on the contrary, you do not have a fixed schedule of less than 8 hours of a day. At the beginning entrepreneurship is more demanding.
- When you think you are going to become a millionaire overnight.
  There are only a few people who have become millionaires in a very short time, however, you have to know and go through the process to understand it. The reality is that it is almost impossible to achieve. For that you have to work very hard and many sacrifices have to be made along the way.
- When you believe that your idea is unique.
  In this era there are no unique ideas, someone else thought of it before you. If you consider that your

idea is unique and no one will copy it, evaluate well if you are going to undertake it or not because it can leave you disappointed if you fail to execute it the way you wanted to.

- When you are not used to failure.

  Most entrepreneurs have failed at least once in their life and it is very difficult to get over the failure and start again. It doesn't mean that if it's your first venture you shouldn't try it. It just means that you should be prepared for failure.

- When you are a conformist.

  A conformist does not fit in the world of entrepreneurship. It can only cover expenses, but it will not generate financial freedom.

- When you don't have a business plan.

  Without a proper execution plan, with clear objectives and defined dates, the best thing to do is NOT to start a business. Most likely, the business will not prosper and will have to be closed soon enough.

- When you are not psychologically prepared for stress and pressure.

  These two words become part of your daily life, there is stress because you have not been able to get paid and you are under pressure because the employees demand their payment. You must be prepared for such circumstances.

All these factors have been pointed out by entrepreneurs who took risks and failed, got back on their feet and now it is just a very bad experience for them which helped them learn and grow.

> "When everything seems to be going against you, remember that the airplane takes off against the wind, not with it.
>
> *Henry Ford*

Experience: I am aware that many of my ventures I should not have started at the first place, failed. Now that I know the best path to follow, it is the one I follow to shape my future ventures. Now what I lack is time, which I am learning to manage in order to cover and achieve more.

Can anyone be an entrepreneur?

The clear answer is yes, anyone can be an entrepreneur; however, not everyone can be a successful one.

You have to understand that entrepreneurship is like other talents, when you have it you exploit it and if you don't have it you acquire it, but there are people who don't have it and will never have it, they should partner with people who will help them in their entrepreneurship journey.

In the case of soccer everyone wants to be Messi, his punch, precision and effectiveness make him unique, adding passion and unique skills is phenomenal. The same happens with singers like Pavarotti in opera, Fredy Mercury, Whitney Houston, Michael Jackson, Luis Miguel or Frank Sinatra to mention a few who have privileged voices because their vocal structure is unique from birth and they enhanced it through practice over time.

In entrepreneurship it is the same, you must have talent for entrepreneurship, be able to handle stress, pressure and everything that comes along the way with entrepreneurship. There are people who are more tolerant and adaptive to change.

> "Do what you do so well that they will want to see it again and bring their friends.
>
> ***Walt Disney***

Experience: In my case it was difficult to find my talent since it was not visible like soccer or singing. I knew that in soccer I had two left feet and in singing, my rooster did it better than me. But I did find unique entrepreneurial skills that I could exploit, and that is what I have been doing after my previous job.

Today I have a technology consultancy with employees who have disabilities, an industrial workshop, a mobile workstation creation workshop, food trucks, etc.

New projects are waiting to be executed as well.

What is the best age for entrepreneurship?

Entrepreneurship can be at any age, there are young entrepreneurs under 15 years old like: Fraser Doherty, founder of SuperJam, Christian Owens, founder of Mac Bundle Box, entrepreneurs under 30 years old like Mark Zuckerberg, creator of Facebook, Steve Jobs, co-founder of Apple, or Marcos Galperín, founder of Mercado Libre or over 30 like Jeff Bezos, founder of Amazon, Jan Koum, creator of Whatsapp or Jack Ma founder of Alibaba.

There is no specific age to become an entrepreneur, but there are statistics on the subject matter suggesting the appropriate ages to take the leap.

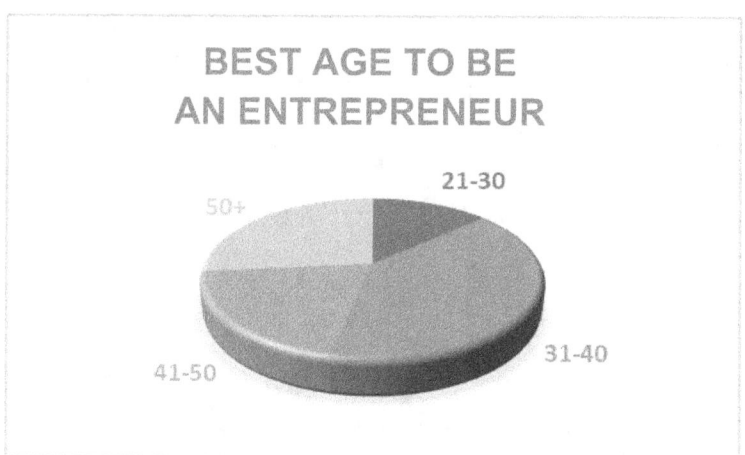

According to the research of "Un café Para emprender", the best age is between 31 and 40 years old, since it is when an entrepreneur has the energy and maturity that will allow him to take his venture towards success. This is not a guarantee since a successful venture depends on many additional factors, but statistically it has been the age range that has been decisive with the most entrepreneurs.

> "It is never too late to embark on a new direction, live a new story or build a new dream.
>
> *Unknown*

Experience: For me the best age is in the 30s, which is when professional and personal maturity kicks in and there is an apt amount of knowledge of what you want to undertake, you have sales skills which can suffice your needs, you know how to capitalize and maintain key contacts.

I insist, this is not the absolute truth, it is just my frame of reference based on my experience and that of many entrepreneurs interviewed.

A good idea

Most people believe that they must keep an idea in a safe deposit box with more than a thousand locks and guards 24x7x365 days.

An idea has zero worth, its value can only be determined after its execution, feedback and turnover of the people assigns the value to an idea.

The idea you have, someone else in the world already had it. Probably none of the people who have that idea have made it real, since they are in the same belief as you and have wasted their time in protecting it, rather than executing it effectively.

Having a good idea is not always enough, you need to find a good opportunity or an unmet need in the market. A good idea is only the first step of something possibly great.

Generally, good ideas are shipwrecked when we don't know how to communicate and execute them effectively. One of the problems is between enthusiasm and arrogance that marks an invisible block to be able to transmit that good idea.

Knowing how to transmit a good idea is very similar to seduction or persuasion. You don't just have to look beautiful, you have to show off, flirt, become interesting, get attention and deliver the thrust.

This process is the one that must be polished, cared for and projected.

It's the first impression that counts: don't waste it.

> "You will never get a second chance to be liked.
>
> *Groucho Marx*

Experience: I have learned that a good idea is not enough, knowing how to transmit an idea, no matter how bad it is, is a great talent indeed. The power of knowing how to convey an idea is better than the idea itself. I learned that one of the most famous soft drink brands in the world sells more because of the way it conveys its product than the product itself.

At a business plan competition in Houston, Texas, I had the opportunity to present a great idea that later became one of my businesses. I was given 4 minutes to convince the judges. I realized that in the competition there were better ideas than mine, however, I won the first place because of the way I presented it, I got to the jury's heart and they congratulated me for that.

Failure; the best teacher

Very few people know that failure teaches you the best lessons.

Many successful entrepreneurs agree that failure has given them the knowledge they needed to be successful. Most people are afraid of failure, not because of the "social issue" rather than the pain involved in accepting failure.

In the entrepreneurial field, failure has many ways of manifesting itself. Some of them are: the loss of sales or business opportunities that vanish, discouraging the entrepreneurs and in less than two years they close their business.

To learn from failure is to give a positive 360 degree turn to a failed venture, to accept that there were failures in the process and that they can be remedied, this is when a failure becomes a mentor and a learned experience. Failure is the most important mentor not only in entrepreneurship, but in life as well.

When you fail, the first thing to avoid is the avalanche of pessimistic thoughts in your head, stop blaming someone else, the environment or emotions for failure. The first thing to do is to take charge and accept responsibility for what happened.

> "You have to taste the failures to enjoy the successes.

Humberto Aguilar

There is no successful entrepreneur who has not failed at some point.

Any entrepreneur before starting a business must be aware of the fact that before success there will be thousands of failures and he must be mentally prepared to be resilient, to get up every time he falls and stand up again to continue towards success.

Experience: I do not know how many times I have failed, how many times I have fallen and how many times I have cried with grief for what I have lost. I have undertaken this journey many times and experienced great positive changes that made me grow beyond expectations.

I understood that every challenge is painful at the beginning, but it can be very rewarding at the end. Once you see the result of an effort, you realize that there were no excuses to be reluctant. Sometimes I wonder why I didn't do it sooner.

Being positive

It is very easy to tell someone not to fret and stay positive, but it is more difficult than it seems. There are a lot of benefits of being positive and many of them intangible, but they reflect in the results.

It is easier for the negative outlook to rip off everything really fast. This is particularly noticeable in the work environment when you see the boss's face unhinged and employees notice that too and ultimately, the environment takes on the seriousness and concern for what he is going to say or what is going to happen. It is also noticeable in home when father is angry and the children notice the frustration through his loud and aggressive tone. When a frustrated person on the street begins to offend a passerby, just like these there are thousands of contagious examples that surround us and effect our mood daily.

Being positive is the ability to perceive the environment or surroundings in a constructive way allowing the impact of only the positive things that can generate something good. It is all about taking the best of reality and cleansing the bad in rivers of goodness.

In business, being positive means developing problem-solving skills that allow us to process complex information with greater clarity.

Being positive is not genetic; it is an acquired trait that is polished over time with conscious efforts, environment and experience. Just like a negative person, a positive one has a gravitational field that attracts others in such a way that they change radically and momentarily.

It is essential for an entrepreneur to be positive despite the circumstances. The mind must be well focused, avoid complaints or any negative attitude, without wasting time.

Benefits of being positive:

- Stress management
  Having positive thoughts controls the level of stress.
- Increased ability to solve problems
  Helps keep the mind focused on solving problems.
- Improved mood
  Being positive keeps bad moods at bay and strengthens group bonds.
- Increases the likelihood of completing projects
  Positive outlook radiates good energy and denotes confidence; a characteristic that clients appreciate.
- Increases creativity
  Research has shown that thinking positive allows us to be more creative and unlocks the creative outlet of an individual.

> "Keep a positive mind and laugh at the negative things.
>
> *Unknown*

Experience: being positive and radiating positive energy to everyone around me has proved to be beneficial not only for me, but also, for everyone around me. Most of the time I would come into the office saying hello, joking, cheering people up, telling some funny experience or just laughing at something I had just seen. Everyone would tell me I was crazy, but they kept coming to my office to distract themselves, de-stress or have fun. Sometimes I think I got paid for making people laugh rather than what I worked for.

I learned that it's easier to move the world while smiling than to try to move the world with anger.

Why does an entrepreneur fail?

The statistics speak for themselves and there is a lot of information about the percentage of failures and successes in entrepreneurship.

According to the financial software company Bloomberg, 75% of new businesses fail in their first three years of life.

There are thousands of reasons why an entrepreneur fails, however, some of the most important ones are.

- Emotions
  Business is not driven by emotions; it is driven by well thought out plans, channels and models.
  It is important to have emotions to start a business, but only if they are used as motivation to push you to make things happen, to run a business especially in the early years you must keep your emotions aside to take practical decisions for better outcomes.
- Lack of experience
  Most of the cases that failed, the entrepreneurs had a fresh idea and motive and they were very excited and dedicated too, however, the lack of experience begins to put obstacles in the way that demoralizes the entrepreneur and end up letting time and petty failures consume them.
- Insufficient capital
  Another factor that has resulted in absolute failure is the lack of money i.e. the project capital to undertake the required operation becomes insufficient, since key economic factors are not

taken into account and big costs are only considered, but the small and miscellaneous costs are usually a big headache that they end up leaving the project unfinished.

- Believing that people think the same way you do
Many times we believe that our tastes are compatible with the tastes of others and we do things that we are sure will be a resounding success, however, the result is a complete failure and brings consequences that are difficult to understand.
- Mismanagement of goods and products
This is where bleeding costs starts to kill the venture because of poor management.
- Commitment
Lack of commitment is a key factor that determines the failure of any venture, no matter how promising it may seem. It is better not to undertake it if you are not fully committed than to leave half of the things unattended.

- Differentiation
  It happens when only preexisting ventures are copied, but there is nothing to distinguish them from others, so a customer will prefer to go with another supplier who can give added value through the differentiation of their products or services than buy from a place that does not offer anything new, unique and valuable.
- Marketing
  Marketing is a factor that is not considered in the budget to give a big push to the venture and this causes a venture to be born weak and lacking visibility.

In summary, all these problems can be prevented with a sound planning, where there are no feelings involved.

> Failure is simply the opportunity to begin again, this time more intelligently.
>
> *Henry Ford*

Experience: I failed in my first ventures due to lack of knowledge, experience and capital to sustain my venture after 6 months, I got discouraged very quickly because I wanted to see profits in the same month I started my venture and I could not understand at that time why an outstanding business idea was not able to generate the desired results.

Even knowing stories of entrepreneurs who have failed for the same reasons, I never understood the fact that, "A person does not learn in someone else's head", until I experienced it myself.

Can you start a business without money?

There are thousands of opinions that indicate that you can do a business without money, however, it all depends on the magnifying glass with which you look at your current state and future prospects.

Every single business requires capital, but this absolute truth is not visible apparently and a person can never know the hidden costs of a venture, until unless experienced such a thing by himself.

The asset that directly supports money is time, the cost of eating is not money, it is time, the cost of dressing is not money, it is time. Time is not a tangible asset that can be exchanged or you can get your precious time back. Therefore, a business requires a person's time, which has an economic value translated into money. Perhaps for this reason those who say that no money is required to create a business have no idea of the value of their time.

You cannot create a business without money "time", but there is a possibility to start a business with very little money.

Many big companies started in a garage "private place where cars are kept" such as:

1. Apple
2. Amazon
3. Disney
4. Harley Davidson
5. Lotus Cars
6. Microsoft

7. Google
8. Mattel
9. YouTube
10. HP Hewlett Packard

These are great companies with great inspirational stories that started with very little budget, but why do people say they started with no money, because they don't pay attention to details.

Starting in a garage also has its costs; the only difference is that, cost will be lower.

All these companies could not afford the monthly expenses of a formal and well established office at the initiation of their entrepreneurship career; however, most of them were supported by their parents, lending them their garage.

Initial cost to start a business in a garage:

Initial cost/person	Cost
Table	$ 100.00
Chair	$ 50.00
Computer	$ 500.00
Desktop	$ 100.00
Stationery	$ 50.00
	$ 800.00

This cost of $800.00 is based on the minimum capital necessary to start working. However, there are concurrent expenses that must be taken into account such as:

Salary	Cost
Jack-of-all-trades	$ 300.00

The first salary that must be covered is the one of the entrepreneur who initially is managing everything on his own and is only surviving with a very meager amount just to eat, without luxuries or any diverse expenses.

And finally the fixed costs:

Monthly Fixed Costs	Cost
Garage	$ 500.00
Internet	$ 50.00
Electricity	$ 50.00
Water	$ 50.00
Gas	$ 20.00
	$ 670.00

In summary, under this magnifying glass we have demonstrated that no business can start without a capital. It doesn't matter who pays for it in the beginning, but you must have capital.

In the case of these aforementioned great brands, they were supported in their beginnings by their relatives and after positioning themselves, they had the opportunity to grow enough to be recognized globally.

> A business is born with an idea strengthened with dreams, and starts to flow with capital.
>
> *Humberto Aguilar*

Experience: In one of my first ventures I thought that by just creating a service company I would not have to spend any money since it was based on teaching people public speaking and other types of coaching. Reality was something else that unfolded later on, although I didn't have an office as such, we did consume stationery, video cameras to record the classes, purchase flights for transportation, rent space for the classes, etc.

It wasn't a big expense, but for the first few months I backed it up with what I earned at my full-time job.

I let myself be carried away by the impulse and a great idea, but I lacked a real planning to start this business and even more to make it grow.

Also, the partners lacked the same interest and commitment I had and the passion I felt for this business.

Partners

The word partner comes from the Latin socius (co-worker). This vocabulary defines a person or individual associated, linked, affiliated, aggregated, colligated, confederated or incorporated with other(s) for some purpose, an individual who is a part of some society or a group of people with the same purpose.

One of the secrets of the success of a partnership is to carefully choose your partner or partners, so that they must have certain characteristics that complement the entrepreneur's shortcomings that you have.

Each partner must cover some basic characteristics and complementary characteristics for the business to function properly.

> "Geography has made us neighbors. History has made us friends. Economics has made us partners, and Necessity has made us allies. Those whom God has so joined together, let not man put asunder.
>
> *John F Kennedy*

How to choose a partner?

1. Chemistry

   Having a good relationship with your partner is indispensable, but having chemistry, supporting, complementing, understanding and following each other is fundamental for a partnership to work.

2. Competencies

   A competent partner with outstanding capabilities who is willing to contribute to the business, and is skilled in what he does.

3. Trust

   A key person who can be trusted blindly as they are important in the transformation and decision making of the company.

4. Complementary

   A person who can develop in other areas where he complements with his/her knowledge and not a partner who does and knows the same things as the main partner, you need a partner who cover ups your deficient areas.

5. Resilient

   Partner with people who have tasted failures, who can get up from any fall and not a partner who runs away at the first problem.

6. Committed

   Partner capable of being there at any time, moment and place without pressure, that is equally committed and invested to the business 100% and more as you are.

7. Contacts

A partner with contacts is a partner that brings potential customers, which is profitable for any business. Networking is the key!

8. Flexible

A partner with flexibility to reach agreements, with reasonable arguments and open to any discussion.

> Trust is earned, respect is given, and loyalty is demonstrated.
>
> ***Unknown***

Experience: In my initial ventures I chose partners with similar characteristics to mine, I wanted them to be the same as me, they did not complement me, and they only matched me. Then I chose my partners because they were better than me, but they didn't complement me, they didn't match me, they only surpassed me. Then I got smarter partners, but they always had limits. Now I get partners who are loyal, capable and hungry to succeed, it has been the best bet ever.

Common mistakes to avoid while choosing a partner:

- A partner is not required for a certain type of business.

    Many times a partner is sought for a business that can be run by a person and it may not be necessary to bring in someone else who will not contribute anything. The fear of entrepreneurship makes new entrepreneurs look for someone to share the responsibility, even if it is not necessary. If the business fails, the responsibility for failure is divided between the two partners and it is easier to blame the other person for the loss as well.

- Lack of contract.

    A venture should never be started without a legal binding or contract, as partners tend to forget the extent of their responsibilities.

    Entrepreneurs mostly think of their partners as gullible beings who would never betray them in any case, which we all know is not true.

- Confusing friendship with partnership

    Many partners enter the business through friendship and know how to manipulate the other person in the name of friendship. However, they confuse friendship with partnership and they are two things that have different connotations and requirements.

Do not do business with friends if the relationship, responsibilities and benefits are not documented in a contract.

- Non-complementary skills
Thinking that having the same skills will be complementary, however, in most ventures different skills are required to complement the shortcomings of one with the strengths of the other.
- Contrasting values
When values contrast between partners it is best not to partner because at first you can tolerate each other, but at some point it will annoy you so much that it will eventually end up in a breakup.

> Be humble to admit your mistakes, smart to learn from them and mature to correct them.

David Fischman

Experience: In my career as an entrepreneur I have been wrong many times, but in one of my businesses I chose a couple of partners that I thought complemented me. Initially I talked to them, told them why I set out to partner with them, told them that the business would be divided fairly equally "so that they would be motivated and give more than 100%" and everything went very well at the beginning. As all businesses do not give profits in the first months and it became more of an expense because I had to contribute from my salary. They started to get discouraged because they were not making a profit. The business demanded more from us and they became discouraged and did not maintain the same interest and momentum that I had. First I had to tell one of them that I no longer wanted to work with her since I ended up doing her part, later on the other partner became irresponsible and in the end I had to tell her that there was no point in continuing with that partnership. I was very frustrated to know that somehow I failed as a partner and I could not maintain a healthy and profitable business. I lost money during the time I was running it, but I gained a lot of experience in the search for a partner.

Systematize your business

Nowadays, a business that is not systematized and automated, rarely survives. Many entrepreneurs only focus on sales as a key factor. However, there is also another factor that has taken a lot of strength with the passage of time and with the advent of technology, which leads to the systematization of a business.

Creating a system refers to establishing channels with well researched order, with the objective of obtaining great results.

When we talk about business systematizing, it refers to creating systems, processes and procedures to complete tasks in a standardized and optimal way. As a company grows, it is not possible to be on top of everything. So, in order to build a successful business, it is necessary to introduce systems and processes that can be automated as much as possible.

Globally recognized companies owe their success to the adoption of systematization in their workflow. Imagine McDonald's, if each of its employees made the burgers the way they wanted. It would not be as successful as it is today. McDonald's not only systematized its business, it patented its hamburger creation system in record time.

Henry Ford (1863 - 1947) was a famous American businessman, the founder of Ford Motor Company. He not only developed the production lines we know today but he systematized his car business also, which earned him the top tier position in his field.

Experience: Like many new entrepreneurs, I also believed that systematization of workflow was not necessary because the company had to grow first. However, when a company grows, it requires the creation of systems that help control and ensure the continuous and balanced growth of the business. I learned this concept through the recommendation of an entrepreneur friend who told me that I needed to adopt systems that would help my business grow in a sustainable manner over time.

Business Plan

It is the recipe that will lead you to success. Creating a good business plan will allow the creation of the business to have as few mistakes as possible.

A business plan can help you get investors who want to be confident that their investment will pay off, or financers who will financially support the entrepreneur.

A business plan will be the tool you use to convince people that working with you is definitely a smart choice.

Most businesses that fail within the first two years are the one that did not have a business plan to follow, no structure, no path, no line drawn to follow through on all the key points to achieve success.

The most successful entrepreneurs, investors and partners do not recommend starting a business without a well-researched plan to back it up.

Currently there is a lot of literature that indicates how to create a business plan, however, the most important points to cover are:

- Executive summary.
  Indicate what the company is, its objectives, product or services, and basic information about the management team, employees, and location of the company. Also include financial information and high-level growth plans if you are planning to get it financed.
- Story

Telling a background story related to your business plan is vital, as it can open investors' hearts and they will want to know more about the project or business.

- Problem to be solved

  A good plan should have a purpose to be solved by the business to be executed.

- Business proposal

  It is the explanation in a clear, supported and attractive way about the results you can offer to your client: how you will help him to reach his goals and how much it will cost him to hire you for that purpose.

- Competition

  Who are they, what are the products and/or services they offer, how long have they been in your area of influence, where are they located, what is their market share, what is their customer typology, what is their pricing policy, what is their marketing strategy, do they sell online, do they engage in promotions or not, do they use social media to publicize their products, do they have a blog to talk to their customers?

- Product or service

  The Product or Service is the means through which a company can satisfy customer needs. It is the materialization or response that a company gives to the real needs of customers. It is important to be able to explain what the product or service to be offered is about.

- Market

  Efforts are made to know the potential customers i.e. the target market and the competitors in that area who are already well rooted. Based on a thorough analysis, it is possible to gain a competitive advantage with a sound marketing strategy.
- Revenue modeling

  Revenue modeling can help understand which channels are the most preferable to build a sustainable revenue generating business. Summing up, how revenue is going to be generated over the period of next 3 years.
- Financial requirement

  How much capital is going to be requested from the investors and how is the expense going to be distributed, it is an essential part of business planning. In the financial plan, all the detailed and quantified information of the plans and objectives that your company is going to undertake must be compiled.
- Work team

  One of the most important elements of your business plan is the section that provides information about why you and your management team are the most qualified individuals to start and run this new venture. This particular section describes the structure of your organization, and when you start off your venture you may also need

to offer incentives to attract qualified personnel as well.

> "Success is not achieved only with special qualities. It is primarily a work record, method and organization.
>
> ***J.P. Sergent***

Experience: I am a staunch believer of the view that no entrepreneur should start a business without a business plan that has been thoroughly drafted and validated by a mentor.

It is extremely important to have this map that will reduce errors on the road to building the new business.

Right place

In an experiment initiated by Washington Post columnist Gene Weingarten, Bell donned a baseball cap and performed as an incognito street musician at the L'Enfant Plaza Metro station in Washington, DC on January 12, 2007. The experiment was videotaped on hidden camera; of the 1,097 people passing by, seven stopped to listen to him and one of the listeners recognized him too. For his nearly 45-minute performance, Bell collected $32.17 from 27 passersby. Three days earlier, he earned considerably more playing the same repertoire at a concert.

One thing that gets a very little attention is the place we are at. No one questions whether it is the right or perfect place for us to develop. We get used to the idea that it is the place where we have to be and we adapt to the situation without questioning anything about it.

Without knowing we fall into conformity and many times we believe that if something bad and unfortunate happens it is because of our incompetence. However, just like the violinist, there are people out there who end up at the wrong place, who are never valued for what they bring to the table just because they are at the wrong place.

It is not the fault of the company or business that hired us to work there, it is our fault that we do not know our worth or how to quantify our effort.

Neither it is the fault of whoever rents us a space to set up a business.

It is only our fault for not analyzing and questioning if what we are setting for is perfectly suited to our interests or not!

> If we are a bigger fish than the pond in which we were bred, instead of adapting to it, we must seek the ocean.
>
> *Paulo Coelho*

Experience: Many times I wanted to adapt to a place out of necessity or fear of rejection. However, time starts to make you uncomfortable and take you out of the place where you are.

I have worked in many companies and I have discovered that there came a time when I was too small for what I wanted to be in my personal and professional life.

I discovered that it was no longer the right place for me and instead of doing anything good, it started to hurt me. I changed my attitude and I stopped liking the place, the environment and everything started to be annoying.

The best thing to do was to quit, leave and look for a better place for me and that's how I recovered my smile and happiness.

Attracting clients

Within the process of growing the venture is the acquisition of customers. In the past, the process was slower because sales agents had to go knocking on doors of businesses, get the right contact, make appointments, understand the potential customer, show the product or service to be sold, apply the necessary psychology to persuade and finally close the deal. Nowadays, the process is much fast and easy, since there are many tech based applications that have made it possible to engage in conversations with clients remotely, through video conferences.

> "90% of selling is conviction and 10% is persuasion
>
> ***Shiv Khera***

There are many strategic techniques to get customers, to name a few:

1. Cold calling: convincing customers through real-time conversations.
2. Inbound marketing: attract the attention of your customers by using interesting content.
3. Display advertising: focus on your target market.
4. SEA advertising: pay-per-click to reach your quality leads immediately.
5. LinkedIn: make new connections to sell more.

6. E-mail Marketing: your potential customers always have your brand in mind.
7. Affiliate Marketing: let other companies help you sell your products.
8. Reviews and testimonials to get new customers.
9. Event marketing: convince potential customers face-to-face.

The power of socializing

Socializing is a life changing skill if learned and used the right way. It is the process by which the human beings learn from their environment, how to live together, language, culture and customs to be able to move in the society.

As societies are diverse and complex, certain phases and levels of relationship are required to conform to that environment.

Both in the work environment and in entrepreneurship, socializing involves studying in depth all the components that strengthen the social circle.

Whoever has the power to socialize is like a chameleon in the jungle; he is only seen and perceived the way he wants to be seen. Today, social media has greatly modified the art of socializing and networking.

There are key points to consider when socializing.

- Create a personal story of sacrifice
- Raise awareness within your social circle
- Show unconditional support towards the community
- Attend meetings
- Be humble

Dark side of entrepreneurship

Entrepreneurship also has a dark side that many people use in order to be "successful" quickly, although not in the best way, leaving aside loyalty, honesty and ethics.

It seems impossible to believe, however, this is more common than we think. There are many entrepreneurs who are devoid of honesty and ethical value; they do a few things out of the way in order to win projects.

Unfortunately this is seen more in Latin American countries; it does happen in the first world countries too, just that they are more cautious.

Some of the most known tricks to be able to win projects are:

- Special parties for the client
  This is a widely used effective strategy, you use your soft skills to manipulate their grateful side and get a solid response back.
- Offer cash for projects
  This trick is one of the oldest and easiest to hide, since a specific amount is agreed for the owner of the project and added to the total cost of the project, which will be delivered in cash or other valuables that is agreed upon between both the parties.
- Over-payments
  They are easier to trace when you are suspicious of someone, but as long as you do not suspect it goes unnoticed normally.

- False quotations
  The famous rule of the 3 quotes, where the same supplier quotes and looks for 2 other allied suppliers and asks them to create a higher quote than the first one to win that project for his own company, in case you decide for the second or third one, the commission is still ready.
- Sex
  Many entrepreneurs use this strategy as a bargaining chip. Nobody notices, it can be done at any time of the day and cannot be traced unless it is through a formal investigation.
- Personalized bribes
  This method applies to houses, cars, trips, etc. that the supplier buys and allows the project owner to use as long as the win-win relationship is maintained.
- Donations
  This is where money laundering is born and is another practical way to buy off project managers.

Obviously this is something that no one writes in a book or for guidelines on strategies, these ways are not good and ethical, but they work in the parallel universe.

> "Genuine sincerity opens people's hearts, while manipulation causes them to close.
>
> *Daisaku Ikeda*

Experience: In my career I had many experiences of suppliers wanting to buy my authorization to accept them in different projects, they would invite me to lunch and take advantage of the meal to earn my support, and on other occasions they were more direct and immediately wanted to bribe me with money, spices or sex. Unfortunately all these tricks that are used do not allow capable, loyal, ethical and moral entrepreneurs to be considered in projects where they can be more effective and even as the owner of the project to shine.

The social game

One of the most important skills that an employee and/or entrepreneur must acquire and polish is how to use the social game to gain advantage.

You can be the best at what you do, the most capable, the fastest, the most honest, the most loyal, however, if you don't have the social skills, you will hardly be able to achieve success, and there are very little chances of making huge profits.

Experience: An excellent teacher and mentor of the mastery once told us in class that profit is 80% social and 20% talent. But success lies in one being the complement of the other.

If you have 20% talent, but no social skill, you are only GURU of the particular field, the smart one, the solver, but you won't be able to get far in your career.

If you have 80% social skills, but lesser talent, you will get very far very quickly, but everyone will realize soon that you can't solve a problem.

If you have 80% social skills and 20% talent, you have the recipe of success.

Although no one knows the absolute truth, this fact is a reference of what great minds have discovered about how important it is to be socially active and balanced.

To know how to play the social game it is important to know:

1. The battlefield
   This means that you must know the place where you are going to develop and also the rules that must be respected. Each place has its own rules to follow. You cannot act in the same way everywhere, the clients you visit or the projects you develop. Try to move with the flow and not against it.
   Only the brave move against the current and the smart ones flow with it.
   Example: Are customers always right?
   The brave ones would say NO
   The smart ones would say ALWAYS
   One study indicates that 95% of respondents say that customers are always right.
   This statistic from a social point of view means that the brave will not get far.

2. The players
   Knowing the players is of utmost importance as it will allow you to have the upper hand in the social game. Before a meeting with clients, or with the different work teams, it is important to study each person you are going to interact with.
   Research the personal and professional side of each person, and use that information to persuade the players.

Example: If you are going to visit a client and he is a car and food lover, the ideal would be to invite him to lunch and before looking to close a contract or service talk about the car he has, the price in the market, power, consumption, updates, etc. This will open the door of friendship and would increase the chances of closing a deal by 35%.

In short, neuroscience says that as human beings we have to belong to a society, that is why we must harness this need of belonging and make the most of every encounter we have with a potential client, business owner or someone who has a project.

Recommendations to reach success faster

One of the things that an entrepreneur must do to get closer to success is to follow in the footsteps of those who have already done what he is currently trying to achieve. It is better to walk on a path that has already been walked than to just build your own from scratch.

Most successful entrepreneurs have followed a very characteristic pattern, which is to copy what other entrepreneurs have done and then add their magic "Their own essence".

Learn to say NO

The mind is wonderful, and it can be manipulated easily. Whether you are an employee or entrepreneur, there is one word that can save you a lot of trouble if you learn to manage it effectively in all areas of your life.

Say NO

Most people commit to doing things they don't really want to do. They are so committed to their society, community, friends, family, supervisors, religion, government, partners, employees, and even to themselves that they would rather sacrifice themselves than utter the most difficult word that has only 1 syllable, 2 letters and that is NO.

This has been demonstrated by neuroscience, the problem lies in the fear of being socially isolated and no longer belonging to a specific social group, however, it has also shown that this fear can be controlled too.

Saying no will prevent an employee and/or entrepreneur from committing to something he does not want to do and will save a lot of time, money, effort and will alienate certain people who need to be kept at bay.

Steps to say NO

1. Know your limits
   You are the one who better understands your limits than anyone else in this world. It is better to say no at the beginning and "look bad", than to look bad because it exceeds your limits.

2. Understand the request
   Effective listening is a remarkable quality that must be developed. In order to understand someone it is necessary to pay attention to the person who wants something from you. Once you understand the request you will be able to prepare your arguments to say no.
3. Say NO
   The best, the shortest and the most painful part is composed of a two-letter word "NO". Just breathe and say no, without including feelings of any kind.
4. Prepare your argument
   Once the goal of saying no is achieved, the argument will be fluid. It should be short with a simple explanation. No, because I can't, No, because I don't want to, No, because I don't have to, No, because I don't have to, No, because no means no.
5. End the conversation
   It is time to thank the other person for consideration and apologize for not being the right time or phase to engage in the said task.

It is not as difficult as it seems, but once you say NO, it will become practical and easy.

Experience: For me, learning to say NO was not very difficult. However, I don't think I've mastered the art of saying no 100% yet.

I used to be dominated by the fear of feeling socially guilty for not helping others with something that I had worked hard to obtain and learn.

I believed that if someone approached me it was because I could be their salvation and that at some point that miracle would come back to me, multiplied by thousands times.

There are many people who take advantage of this vulnerability of the human brain and exploit it for their convenience.

> "It is very difficult to detect the wolf in sheep's clothing among the flock.
>
> ***Humberto Aguilar***

After years of experiencing this abuse by many people, I decided to say no. The first time I said no to someone, that person stopped talking to me. The second time I said no, they told me that if I didn't help I wouldn't get anything because God would punish me, and so on and so forth I became an expert and at the same time created a reputation. Today, thanks to all the abusive people, I learned to say no.

Public Speaking

One of the factors that bring an employee or an entrepreneur closer to success is the art of public speaking.

Public speaking is not a skill that we are born with; we must develop it over time. We are all capable of it, just by using the right tools to master it.

Public speaking has as many benefits for an employee as it does for an entrepreneur, among those benefits are:

1. Self-confidence
   It is much more important than what it projects; our level of self-confidence determines how we view ourselves.
2. Communication skills
   Ability to elaborate, send and receive information oriented to specifically defined objectives, in order to obtain a favorable result.
3. Reasoning
   Intellectual and logical process of human thinking which allows the delivery of arguments in an organized and easily perceivable manner.
4. Leadership
   A person's ability to influence, motivate, organize and carry out actions to achieve his goals.
5. Better perception
   The way the brain interprets the signals it receives through the sensory and motor system of our body to form an impression of reality.

> If you have a voice and you are heard, you better say something worthwhile and change someone's life.
>
> *Unknown*

To be a good entrepreneur public speaking is a must have skill public, which will be of great help in customer connections, sales, employee motivation, follow-up and training.

Experience: Learning to speak in public has allowed me to grow professionally by 200%. It has taught me that you can be wrong ideologically, but if you have a good argument and know how to communicate it, people will believe you. It gave me self-confidence, courage and the ability to express anything and anywhere in an assertive way.

Create your habits

It is very well known that habits define people. In short, your habits define who you are.

Habits are behaviors that are performed repeatedly until they become part of a person's daily life. This repetition makes habits an involuntary reflex of a person.

Studies from Duke University indicated that, "habits account for approximately 40% of our behaviors on any given day." In other words, almost half of what we do in a day, we do automatically and repeatedly because we always do it that way.

Advantages

The advantage of having a habit is that the brain expends less energy and cognitive resources while performing it. When a habit is healthy it enhances other habits and resources that normally accompany positive outcomes.

Disadvantages

The disadvantage of having a habit is that, if a habit is unhealthy, it is like a drug that brings negative consequences to your physical, mental, emotional and social state.

Tell me what habits you have and I will tell you who you are.

Create a good habit

A well-focused person changes his habits in order to improve in various aspects of his life, however, it is not an easy job to make a change of habits, or create a new habit.

To create a new habit it is necessary to pay the price of repeating it as many times as necessary until the body records it in its memory, that particular sequence and the pattern to do it.

Researchers

There is a belief that a new habit is formed in 21 days. This belief is due to plastic surgeon Maxwel Maltz, in the 1950s, who began to notice a strange pattern among his patients. According to his observations, it took them about 21 days to get used to seeing their new face.

These experiences gained by the surgeon made him think that the behavioral adaptation period was 21 days.

Maxwel Maltz tried it himself and concluded that the 21 days worked for him as well.

Maltz wrote "These, and many other observed phenomena; tend to show that a minimum of about 21 days is required for an old mental image to be replaced with a new one."

With this data Maltz started the 21-day belief and influenced almost all major "self-help" authors, and from this the famous 21-day law was born.

In 2009, Phillippa Lally, a health psychology researcher at University College London, published a study in the European Journal of Social Psychology in which she calculated an average of more than 2 months before a new behavior becomes involuntary, which is almost 66 days.

This acquisition of a new habit can vary widely depending on the behavior, the person and the circumstances.

Entrepreneurial habit

According to several successful entrepreneurs it is important to have certain habits that add up to attract success.

While it is true that entrepreneurship is not easy, it is also true that successful entrepreneurs have some habits in common that led them to achieve what they have today, speaking of economy, fame, presence and comfort.

To have these habits it was necessary to include passion, discipline and dedication to the formula.

Some common habits that successful entrepreneurs have in common are:

1. They start their day very early
2. They create a daily plan and follow it.
3. They exercise
4. They educate themselves daily
5. They live a disciplined life

Perfection is the enemy of an entrepreneur

Many entrepreneurs have this characteristic of wanting to do things perfectly, they would never dare to launch a product or service if the quality or design did not turn the way they had envisioned in their mind.

It always works against any entrepreneur since they never have a real deadline for the release of their product or service and it only remains in mental sketches.

Perfectionism is a double-edged sword, on one hand, although we know that nothing is 100% perfect but still we are in search of this perfection which brings many problems because it is not achievable and this makes many entrepreneurs get frustrated who quit because they do not feel confident. On the other hand, the pursuit of perfection makes certain entrepreneurs stand out from others because of their innovative products or services that change the way we look at life.

> "Perfection is a polished collection of errors."
>
> *Mario Benedetti*

Experience: Perfection in my first ventures worked against me and I found it very difficult at the time of my first releases because in my eyes they were not perfect enough to be shown to the world. I always believed that people would realize that something was missing, but that was only the product of my mind, not the minds of others.

Now, I have learned to plan my releases in parts and that's how I manage it and this mantra has worked for me. I do try to make it as perfect as possible, but I don't get frustrated if it's not. The perfection parameter is no longer 100%, with 80% you can go for the release.

Employee or Entrepreneur
Which one gives you financial freedom?

Financial freedom does not depend 100% on the income you earn, whether working for a company or owning one. Financial freedom is based on different variables; income is only one variable that helps define financial freedom. Financial freedom should not be related to success. There are many successful people out there who do not have a penny in their wallet.

There are more employees in the world who are financially free than most of the entrepreneurs.

We are surrounded by ignorant and influential people who base their income on manipulating the minds of people who want to be millionaires and have a financially solvent life, such people use expensive but effective advertising gimmicks to make the world believe that you must follow their advice to become a millionaire.

Financial freedom, according to people who are financially free must add up the following variables.

Financial Freedom = Finances + Happiness + Time

1. Finances
    It is the way in which a person manages his money in the right way.
2. Happiness
    The brain's interpretation of feeling excited about well-being, joy or happiness.

3. Time
   The measurement of the orderly continuation and sequence of events through "past, present and future" changes.

Other variables that do not enter into the **financial freedom** formula, but are extremely important:

- Health
  The World Health Organization says that health is a state of complete physical, mental and social well-being.
- Love
  The most important element of the human life, the feeling that moves the internal fibers of the organism. The motivational element that allows us to do difficult things.

> "Take into account that great love and great achievements involve great risk.
>
> *Dalai Lama*

Experience: Financial Freedom is just a marketing device to sell books, courses and trips. It serves to motivate people to become millionaires through entrepreneurship.

In this world of entrepreneurship I have met several double-faced and double-minded people who boast about luxuries they cannot afford or fake their lives in front of people.

Financial freedom exists, but not in the way that social media try to portray it to common people.

If you want to be financially free, create a strategy, follow a plan, prepare yourself, learn from the best, from those who have already achieved what you want to achieve and pay the price.

You can be financially free, being an employee or being an entrepreneur. It doesn't matter which source you choose to earn income, but it does matter how you manage the formula of your life.

You will be attacked by thousands of pessimistic thoughts that will invite you to give up when you are just a few steps away from success. Don't be influenced by this negative and conformist source. Go ahead, look for your inner talents and execute your plan with passion.

Success is closer than you think.

> "Whether you think you can or think you can't, you´re right.
>
> *Henry Ford*

www.ingramcontent.com/pod-product-compliance
Lightning Source LLC
Chambersburg PA
CBHW071412210526
45465CB00001B/355